published in the united states by kaleidoscope kids llc

visit us at www.readkaleidoscope.com

kaleidoscope, *kids bibles reimagined*

library of congress cataloging-in-publication data is available upon request
ISBN
hardback: 978-1-7360171-9-7

cover art by becca godfrey @becca.godfrey
logo design by morgan carter @bymorgancarter
editing by bethany denton @betdenton

To Carolina, Kellen, YaYa, Sissy, and AJ.
Thank you for helping me create these drawings.
I pray that you always remember how God loves
us through this son, Jesus, and that your life can
show His amazing love and grace to others.

WELCOME TO KALEIDOSCOPE

First of all, thank you for picking up a copy of Kaleidoscope! We are glad to have you. In the following pages, you'll experience the Bible in a whole new way.

Kaleidoscope was borne from the need to provide a fun, engaging, age-appropriate retelling of the Bible for elementary-aged children to transition them from "little kid" Bibles to adult translations.

At Kaleidoscope, we are producing single volumes for every book of the Bible. They're designed to read like chapter books, so you'll turn pages and look forward with anticipation to the next volume.

But don't let the fact that we are focused on kids deter you if you are a "big kid!" Good children's books are almost always as good for adults as they are for kids.

Get excited! In the pages that follow, you'll see God's wonderful good news. Our prayer is that His kindness, gentleness, and love will melt our hearts and make us more like Jesus.

The Kaleidoscope Team

Kaleidoscope is such a great tool for parents who are committed to discipling their kids. *Live in Love* is no exception. It's perfect for the reader in your home, and works great for reading aloud with your not-quite-readers as well. The content is theologically sound and the style is winsome and clever. Rest assured, you'll be thankful you invested in this resource.

-Ryan "Coat" Coatney, Founder of Cross Formed Kids

"Every minute He gives you is a chance to live in His love." What a beautiful invitation to those that follow Jesus! But living in love is sometimes easier said than done! Thankfully, James and Peter have plenty to say to encourage as we grow—things they learned from Jesus Himself! And this Kaleidoscope volume will give growing Bible readers plenty to think, talk, and pray about as they follow Jesus and learn to live in love.

-Sara Lubbers, author of *Always Love*

Kaleidoscope's aim is big — to help kids see how all the stories in the Bible comprise one grand, beautiful story of redemption. As a parent, Bible teacher, and church planter, I can't commend this approach to Bible study enough.

-Amy Gannett, founder of Tiny Theologians and author of *Fix Your Eyes: How Our Study of God Shapes Our Worship of Him*

As a mom, I longed for a kid's Bible that would keep our children engaged while offering a faithful account of the stories in Scripture. Kaleidoscope is entertaining, responsible, and gospel driven!

-Hunter Beless, Executive Director of Journeywomen

My son loves reading Kaleidoscope because he learns new details about old Bible stories and some new stories he has never heard before. As a mom, I love how Kaleidoscope carefully explains tricky passages while connecting each story to the bigger story of the Bible.

-Maggie Combs, author of *Motherhood Without All the Rules* and *Unsupermommy*

CREATORS

Emily Pressley is an Assistant Principal in Denver, CO. She has a BA from Anderson University in South Carolina and an MA from the University of Colorado. When she's not writing or teaching or reading, you can find her adventuring with family and friends, hiking up a mountain, or cooking food that's way too complicated for her tiny kitchen.

Hillary Evans is a high school art teacher with an Art Education degree from Anderson University and a Master's in Studio Art from NYU. As a mother of two, she fills her days with coffee, crayons, and imagination. Her husband, Tommy, supports her creative endeavors and is the love of her life. Her favorite form of expression is painting with a new enthusiasm for digital drawing.

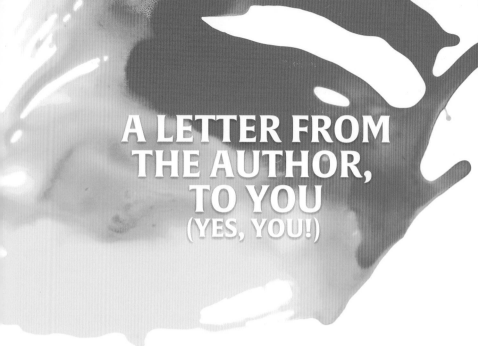

A LETTER FROM THE AUTHOR, TO YOU
(YES, YOU!)

Dear Reader,

I love letters. I love sending them. I love receiving them. I love writing them. I love reading them.

On my shelf, I have a book about famous letters. Charlotte's Web author E.B. White wrote to a reader in 1973:

Hope is the thing that is left to us, in a bad time.

In a large box, I have saved dozens of sweet letters from family and friends. In December of 2017, my dad wrote:

It is always exciting when your birthday comes around because it means only a couple weeks until I get to see you!

In this book, you'll learn about three letters that are found in the New Testament of the Bible. These letters were sent by early Christian leaders: James, the half-brother of Jesus, and Peter, a disciple of Jesus. These letters were sent to many cities around the Mediterranean Sea.

These are good letters. Very good letters. They teach us about the men who wrote them: James and Peter. They teach us about the people who read them: early Jewish and Gentile Christians. And most importantly, they teach us about Jesus: how much He loves us, and how He wants us to live.

As much as I love letters, the excitement I feel when I read a letter doesn't come close to the excitement that early Christians would have felt when hearing these letters read aloud for the first time.

Put yourself in their sandals and imagine: a man who knew Jesus—who walked with Him and spoke with Him and ate with Him and heard Him teach and witnessed His miracles and watched Him suffer and die and saw Him risen again—sent you a letter. (Yes, you!)

You would listen carefully, hardly moving, breathing as quietly as possible, so as not to miss a single, precious word. At some words, you'd smile. At other words, you'd cry. Every word would remind you of how much Jesus loves you, and how He wants you to live.

I'm so glad you're here. I can't wait for us to learn more about these letters, together.

Love,
Emily

TABLE OF
CONTENTS

INTRODUCTION TO JAMES   1

A JOYFUL GREETING   3
    JAMES 1:1

JOY WHEN YOUR FAITH IS TESTED   5
    JAMES 1:2-18

LISTENING & DOING   11
    JAMES 1:19-27

DON'T PLAY FAVORITES   15
    JAMES 2:1-13

TRUE FAITH   19
    JAMES 2:14-26

THE POWER & DANGER OF WORDS   23
JAMES 3:1-12

HEAVENLY WISDOM, HOLY FRIENDSHIP,   27
& A RIGHTEOUS JUDGE
JAMES 3:13-4:12

THE FUTURE IS GOD'S   31
JAMES 4:13-5:12

PRAY ALWAYS   35
JAMES 5:13-20

INTRODUCTION TO 1ST PETER   39

A RICH GREETING   43
1 PETER 1:1

HOPE IS ALIVE!   47
1 PETER 1:3-12

SO NOW...   49
1 PETER 1:13-2:3

WHAT GOD IS BUILDING   53
1 PETER 2:4-10

FREE SERVANTS   57
1 PETER 2:11-3:12

FAITH IN SUFFERING   63
1 PETER 3:13-22 & 4:12-19

TO LIVE GOD'S WAY   67
1 PETER 4:1-11

TO THE SHEPHERDS & THE SHEEP   71
1 PETER 5:1-11

INTRODUCTION TO SECOND PETER   75

A SHORT GREETING   79
    2 PETER 1:1-2

GOD'S GRACE LEADS TO GODLINESS   81
    2 PETER 1:3-15

THIS IS HOW WE KNOW   85
    2 PETER 1:16-21

THE DANGER OF FALSE TEACHERS   89
    2 PETER 2:1-22

THE LORD'S DAY IS COMING   93
    2 PETER 3:1-13

UNTIL THEN...   97
    2 PETER 3:14-18

INTRODUCTION TO JAMES

Did you know that on Inauguration Day in the United States, the outgoing President leaves the incoming President a letter? Some Presidents have shared with us what these letters say. Here are a few lines from President George W. Bush's letter to President Barack Obama:

There will be trying moments. The critics will rage. Your "friends" will disappoint you. But, you will have an Almighty God to comfort you, a family who loves you, and a country that is pulling for you, including me.

President Bush wanted President Obama to know that his job wouldn't be easy, but that it would be worth it. James also wanted the readers of his letter to know that their job wouldn't be easy, but that it would be worth it.

1

James was the half-brother of Jesus. While the two men shared Mary as their mother, Joseph was the father of James, and God was the Father of Jesus. Earlier in the New Testament, we learn that James did not believe his brother was God. In fact, he mocked Him, as it is written in Mark 3:21: "He is out of His mind."

But as only Jesus can, and as He often does, He changed James's heart. After Jesus rose from the dead, He spoke to His brother.

The Bible doesn't tell us much about that moment, but we know it changed James's life forever. He is now known as one of the three pillars of the Church, which means he was a leader in the early Christian Church. He was also a teacher early Christians listened to for direction for how to live lives that honored Jesus. And you know what?

Christians today listen to James for the same reason.

James wrote one book of the Bible, this letter to early Christians. These Christians were Jewish by birth, like Jesus. But unlike many Jews of their time, they believed that Jesus was their Savior. Their faith eventually led them to move away from their homes in Israel as other groups of people mistreated them. In doing so, they scattered to different cities around the Mediterranean Sea.

This move, however, did not make their lives much easier. They'd lost their homes. Most of them were poor. Hunger was a daily reality.

But God's people knew their hope was in someone bigger, and so much better. James's letter reminded the believers of this hope, and taught them how to live faithfully.

A JOYFUL GREETING

James 1:1

Most letters today begin with something like this:

Dear _____,

But in ancient times, letters began like this:

From _____,

Then, the author addressed who the letter was for. Next came a short greeting and a blessing.

And that's exactly how James began his letter...

From James, a servant of God and of Jesus Christ the Lord, to the twelve scattered tribes of Israel: Hello! Joy to you!

Kaleidoscope Corner
Ancient Letters

Letters in the ancient world were delivered by trusted friends or family members traveling from one place to another. Letters like James and 1 and 2 Peter, which were written to entire communities, would have been delivered to one location, and then the next, and then the next.

Most people in the early days of the church couldn't read or write, so when a letter arrived, everyone gathered together to hear the letter read aloud by one of the few people who could read.

Open your Bible to James chapter 1, and read verses 1 through 18 aloud to someone: a parent, a sibling, or a friend. How do you think the early Christians felt when they heard these words? Which words would comfort and encourage them? Which words would challenge them? Why?

JOY WHEN YOUR FAITH IS TESTED

James 1:2-18

Speaking of joy, when hard times test your faith,
I want you to think of these trials as joy!
When your faith is tested, you grow in patience.
As your patience grows, your faith becomes strong.
And with strong faith,
you're not missing out on anything.

What joy!

Do you need wisdom?
Ask God.
He pours it out so generously, it overflows.
And when you ask Him, remember:
Strong faith.
Don't doubt.
Doubters are like waves in the sea,
tossed back and forth by the wind.

5

Most other letters in the New Testament open with thanksgiving or praise, and updates about people and places.

Not James.

Right away, he talks about the very thing all his readers had on their mind.

In those days, being a Christian was dangerous. The people James wrote to were treated harshly for their faith, had to leave their hometowns, and were scattered throughout cities around the Mediterranean Sea for their safety.

But moving didn't solve all their problems. Their faith in Jesus was seen as a threat by many Jewish leaders in their new cities who didn't believe Jesus was God's son. So, they faced hard times, grew hungry, and were often homeless.

Can you imagine someone, like James, telling you that you should think of the hunger in your stomach or your fear for your safety as joy?

Remember: James had the same hunger. And the same fear. And he knew Jesus like few people did. He walked with Him and spoke with Him and ate with Him and heard Him teach and witnessed His miracles and watched Him suffer and die and saw Him rise again.

And he was confident that the hunger and the fear and the pain would lead them all to a stronger faith, knowing that God would provide all they needed. This faith, he said, would create joy.

Trials can look different for each of us: sickness, loneliness, disappointment, and sadness. Maybe you've faced these kinds of trials. The next time you feel the sting of embarrassed disappointment on your cheeks, or the ache of loneliness in your heart, will you believe that it can lead you to a stronger faith? Can you think of it as joy?

Here's the key: disappointment, loneliness, hunger, and suffering; Jesus faced them all for you so that He could tell you that life with God is joy. When we experience the same things Jesus did, we have an opportunity not to despair, but to grow closer to the heart of God.

> Let the poorest among us turn to God in his hunger,
> because loss is a test.
> Let the richest among us turn to God in his excess,
> because success is a test.
> And let none of us dare say that God is tempting us,
> because a test alone does not tempt.

Wisdom reminds us that we can rest in the fact that, though we're being tested, God is still in control. Faith reminds us that He is working all things for His glory, and for our good.

And that's why Christians can say with confidence that trials are a joy. A gift, even. James clearly knew this as he ended this section of his letter in this way:

> Every single good thing given in this world is
> a gift from above.
> The giver is our loving Father of Lights.
> His sun casts out all shadows,
> and the Son drives away all darkness.
> He gives us His light,
> and we are like the first fruits of the harvest,
> who waited while the rains pooled and the winds blew;
> and at the right time, blossomed through broken ground
> as the first believers in Jesus.
>
> He has come, and given us salvation.
> He is making us new.

LISTENING & DOING

James 1:19-27

James told his fellow Christians that they were the "first fruits" of the harvest.

First fruits are, well, just what they sound like! You might wait all winter to see the first of the summer fruit sprout from the vine. These fruits taste especially good and give you a hint of what's to come!

This meant these Christians were both an offering of thanks for what God had already done through Jesus, and a promise of what was—and is—to come. So how, then, should they live? James knew the responsibility was great, and gave them advice in the rest of the chapter.

> Believe me, family.
> Listen first.
> Choose your words carefully.
> Don't turn to anger.
> Our anger isn't a place where
> God's righteousness grows.

James wanted his family to hear God's voice, and to be known as a people who wanted to learn and grow. But he didn't stop there...

Listen.
But don't just listen.
Do.
If someone looks at their reflection in a mirror and sees their brown eyes and brown hair, but they walk away and believe that they have blue eyes and blonde hair, they're lying to themselves.

And if someone listens to God's Word and hears the beauty of His perfection,
but walks away
believing they are already holy,
exactly as they are,
they're lying to themselves, too!

But whoever listens to God's Word
and hears the beauty of His perfection,
and knows that they are only truly free
when they follow God's law,
they are blessed with the light of truth.

It may seem strange that James describes following the law as freedom. But God's law teaches us the right way to live. And when we live rightly, we are freed from sin and death so that we can live in love.

Love.
This is doing what God wants.
Take care of widows, who have lost their husbands.
Take care of orphans, who have no parents.
Love those who have been forgotten,
and who have forgotten what love is.
Listen.
Do.
Love.

DON'T PLAY FAVORITES

James 2:1-13

Imagine a poor person and a rich person
come to your party.
You say to the rich person,
"Come sit right up here, in the best seat!
You are most welcome!"
And you say to the poor person,
"I think there's a place for you in the back,
or how about right here on the floor?"

Dear family, that's not what God wants.
That's not who God is.
He's turning the whole world upside down with His love.
The poor, by God's mercy,
will be rich in His kingdom.

James was reminding the early Church that they are the poor ones. Many were poor in how little they owned, and they were all poor in spirit, unable to save themselves from their sin that separated them from God. In the same way, we are also poor in spirit. When we understand how undeserving we are of God's love, we get the power to gently love one another.

When asked what the most important commandment was, Jesus said, "You shall love the Lord your God with all your heart, with all your soul, and with all your mind." He went on, saying, "a second is like it: you shall love your neighbor as yourself." (Matthew 22:36-38) So, if you do not live in love toward others, you are actually breaking God's law.

God's law is clear: playing favorites is a sin.
If you love your rich neighbor,
but you don't love your poor neighbor,
you've broken God's law.

But because of Jesus, mercy beats judgement!
So live like who you are:
people who have been shown mercy.

Since sin first came into the world, none of us have been able to keep the law perfectly. But when you follow Jesus, He has already paid the price for your law-breaking ways.

And when we see that Jesus kept the law perfectly for us... then, and only then, can God's law bring freedom to our lives.

So our job isn't to ignore the law, but to live our lives by it because the law is all about love.

Jesus died in love for us so that we can live in love for others.

Kaleidoscope Corner
James and The Sermon on the Mount

Does this chapter of James sound familiar? The greatest number of words we have recorded from Jesus's time on earth are from the Sermon on the Mount, where He taught a great crowd.

In your Bible, read James 2:13. Then, read Matthew 5:7. Now read James 2:14-16, and Matthew 7:21-23.

What did James know about Jesus? How did Jesus's teachings shape James's teachings?

TRUE FAITH

James 2:14-26

James then explains what true faith *doesn't* look like:

Suppose you know someone who's hurting.
They don't have warm clothes, or enough food to eat.
If you say to them, "I wish you well," but don't give them a
coat or some bread, have you served them at all?
Have you shown your faith?
Have you lived in love?

You say that you believe there is only one true God.
Do you know who else believes that?
Demons.
And they're terrified of God!

Faith—by itself—isn't enough.
Works—by themselves—aren't enough.

To get it right,
you need faith that spills over into good works.

Saying you have faith, without doing any good works, is like wanting Jesus to save you, but then refusing to live as a member of His kingdom.

Likewise, saying, "I do lots of good things, so I don't need Jesus," is like putting yourself in the place of God. You can't make up your own rules for life. That's God's job alone.

James ends this chapter by giving two examples from the Old Testament of what true faith looks like:

Remember Abraham?
He didn't live a perfect life.
He broke God's law again and again by lying.
But he had true faith.
And when God told him to sacrifice Isaac,
his only son,
he was ready to obey.
He was saved by faith alone,
and his works showed how true his faith was.

Remember Rahab?
She didn't live a perfect life either.
She broke God's law again and again by treating more
than one man like her husband.
But she had true faith.
And when the Israelites needed her protection,
she was ready to serve.
She was saved by faith alone,
and her works showed how true her faith was.

A body without a spirit is dead.
And faith without works is dead, too.

THE POWER & DANGER OF WORDS

James 3:1-12

If you want to teach others about God,
know that this is a great responsibility!
So, be careful what you say.

If your tongue is under control,
you'll keep your whole body in line.
A massive horse is directed by
the tiny bit between its teeth.
An entire ship is turned by
the small rudder on its stern.
One flyaway spark
can set a whole forest on fire.
And one careless word
can cause pages and pages of ruin.

Have you ever heard the saying "sticks and stones may break my bones, but words will never hurt me?" It's a lie. Words have enormous power, and can be dangerous. Once words fly over our lips, we have little control over the damage they might cause. Though the tongue is very small, it can literally change the whole world.

Our words praise our Father in Heaven with one breath, and curse people with another.
Dear family, it shouldn't be this way.
Does one stream flow with both fresh and salt water?
Does one tree grow both olives and figs?

Sometimes our words show our sinful nature. And sometimes they reflect our perfect Creator. So ask God to teach you how to talk. Ask Him every day to add wisdom to your words.

Kaleidoscope Corner
James's Audience

If we lose sight of grace, James's letter can seem like a list of rules that we couldn't possibly keep. So it's important to keep the original readers in mind: faithful Christians. They had already been deeply changed by the love of Jesus, so much that they knew He was worth giving up anything for—their homes, jobs, and sometimes even their earthly families.

As you learn about James's letter, remember that it's not a list of rules to follow to *earn* Jesus's love. That's impossible! Instead, his letter is a picture of what our lives should look like when we understand how good Jesus has been to us. It's a picture of what it looks like to live in love.

In your Bible, read James 3:1-12. Then read Jesus's words in John 12:44-46. What changes in our hearts when we believe in Jesus? How does living in the light of God's love change the things we do and the words we speak?

HEAVENLY WISDOM, HOLY FRIENDSHIP, & A RIGHTEOUS JUDGE

James 3:13-4:12

Where does your wisdom come from?
Earthly wisdom brags.
It thinks it has everything figured out.
But it leads to a spiral of jealousy
and the darkness of selfishness
and the chaos of fighting.

Heavenly wisdom rests in God.
It knows that only God has everything figured out.
This wisdom loves peace,
is gentle,
shows mercy,
and blooms with good fruit.

Earthly wisdom *thinks* it has all the answers. Heavenly wisdom *knows* that only God can give answers. Heavenly wisdom reminds us how much God has done for us.

Do you know why you don't have heavenly wisdom?
It's not because you can't have it.
Instead, it's because you don't ask God for it.

Or perhaps you do ask, but for the wrong reasons,
like when you just want to look
smart and clever for your friends.

But when you're more worried about friendship with the
world than friendship with God, you betray Him.
You're acting like His enemy.

Remember, the real enemy is the devil.
Stand firm against him, and he will run away.
With clean hands and pure hearts,
move humbly toward God.
He'll lift you up and hold you close.

No matter how good the gifts of the world may seem, they
are nothing compared to the gifts of the Lord. Find a holy
friendship with our good God, and hold onto it with all
you've got.

Don't speak badly about each other.
When you say evil words about someone,
you're making yourself a judge.
And who decided that you should be a judge?
Only God created the world.
Only God created the law.
And only God will judge righteously.

One way to show the world the grace and beauty of God is
to seek peace with everyone and let God be in charge. May
the peace we build with one another show the world what
God has done for us.

THE FUTURE
IS GOD'S

James 4:13-5:12

Do you ever think to yourself:
"Tomorrow we'll go here and the next day we'll do this?"

Friends, be careful.
Life does not always go according to our plans!
Our plans can seem as short-lived as the morning fog
that drifts away by noon.

So instead, imagine your future like this:
If the Lord wants, then we'll go here or do this.

The future isn't ours. Instead, it belongs to God. Make plans, but always remember who's in charge. Hold your plans for the future with open hands, and know that only God's hands are strong enough to hold all of our days.

James goes on to teach those who were wasting their time, pretending like they were in charge of the world:

> Are you rich, boastful in your greed
> while you steal from your workers?
> Be careful.
> Life is short, earthly treasures rot,
> and judgement is certain.
>
> Instead of the luxury that you're used to,
> you're heading toward death.

James isn't saying that having money is sinful, but that hoarding money, and treating others poorly, most certainly is. James knew that some wealthy land owners weren't paying the workers who'd planted seeds or harvested crops all year long.

The rich were getting richer, and the poor were getting poorer. This, surely, isn't what living in love looks like.

James finishes this part of his letter by reminding us that we actually do know one thing about the future:

> Are you tired of seeing injustice and brokenness?
> Be patient.
> Just as the farmer knows
> that the early rains water the seeds,
> and the late rains water the crops,
> we know that life is short,
> and rescue is coming!
> God is powerful.
> God is kind.
> Our hope is in Him.

PRAY ALWAYS

James 5:13-20

Is life difficult? Pray to God.
Is life good? Praise God.

Are you sick?
Go to the church leaders and ask them to pray.
Believe that Jesus wants to heal you.

Have you sinned?
Tell someone about it,
pray with each other,
and know that you are forgiven.

Healing is both inside and out.

Sickness isn't always caused by sin, but sickness is a painful, physical reminder that the world is not as it should be. Sickness shows us our weakness. But we can praise God for this reminder, because His strength is seen most clearly when we compare it with our weakness.

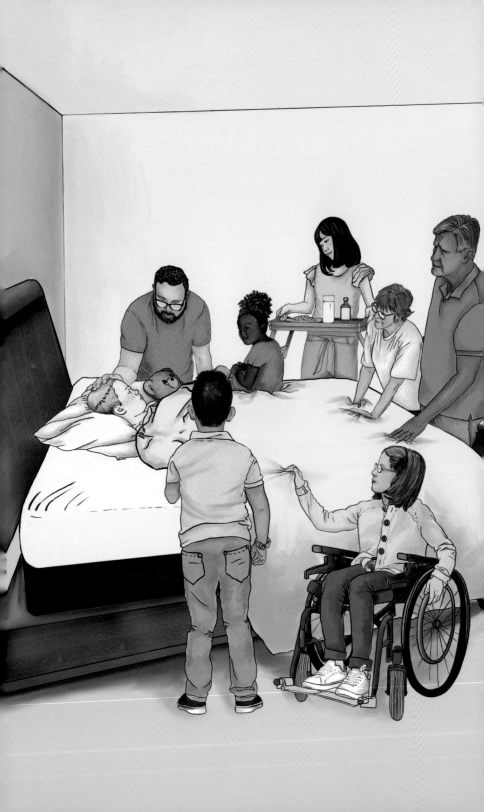

Remind yourself of this beautiful truth, and remind each other:

> If anyone forgets the truth, go tell him!
> Remind him what's true and beautiful.
> And if he stops his wandering,
> know that you've rescued him
> from the pain of destruction.

When we remember the great gifts we've been given, we live differently.

Because of our faith in Jesus, we can have joy when our faith is tested.

Because of our faith in Jesus, we listen to His word and we do what it says.

Because of our faith in Jesus, we take care of each other, especially the poor and sick.

Because of our faith in Jesus, our words encourage and inspire.

Because of our faith in Jesus, we humbly ask for wisdom from heaven and put our future in His hands.

Because of our faith in Jesus, we pray always.

And because of our faith in Jesus, we live together in love. As we do, may our love for each other show the world our love for God.

INTRODUCTION TO 1ST PETER

Before he was President of South Africa, Nelson Mandela was arrested and thrown in jail because he spoke out against his government's treatment of black South Africans. From jail, he wrote in a letter to his children:

I do not know, my darlings, when I will return.
You will remember that in the letter I wrote in 1966 I told you that the white judge said I should stay in jail for the rest of my life.
It may be long before I come back. It may be soon.
Nobody knows when it will be.

Mandela went to jail because he took a stand for what he knew was right, even when he knew it meant that he would suffer because of it. Almost two thousand years before that, some early Christian leaders also went to jail because they took a stand for what they knew was—and is—right, even though they knew it meant they would suffer.

Peter was one of those Christians.

Peter wrote this first of two letters to early Christians who were suffering because they believed that Jesus was both fully God and fully man, and was their Savior. Some of them went to jail because of their beliefs, Peter included. (More on that in the next section.)

Like James, Peter gives his readers a lot of instructions about how to live a life that glorifies God. And Peter also teaches them a lot of Christian theology, which is the study of and beliefs about the faith.

Sometimes you'll read or hear Peter called Simon Peter. That's because the name Peter was born with was Simon. When Jesus called Simon to follow Him, He gave him a new name: Peter. (You can read about this moment in your Bible in John 1:35-42.)

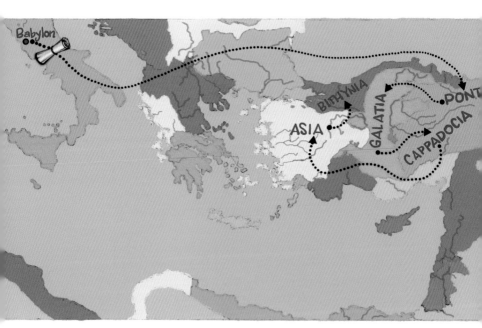

First Peter is a special type of letter, known as a circular letter. Instead being written to just one person or one place, it was circulated to many different people and cities.

Like James, Peter also became known as one of three pillars of the Church. Do you remember what that means? He was a leader in the early church. (If you're curious, the third "pillar" is John, and he also wrote some very good letters in the Bible.)

While James wrote his letter mostly to early Jewish Christians who had been driven out of their homes in Israel and scattered around the Mediterranean Sea, Peter wrote to non-Jewish (called Gentile) Christians. They were also suffering for their faith, losing jobs and money, and often didn't have enough to eat or drink.

Even though Peter would have grown up believing that Gentiles were not God's chosen people, he wrote to his Gentile brothers and sisters as equals in the faith. God had a plan to welcome the Gentiles all along, and that plan was Jesus.

For Peter, who walked with Him and spoke with Him and ate with Him and heard Him teach and witnessed His miracles and watched Him suffer and die and saw Him risen again...Jesus changed everything, because Jesus came for everyone!

A RICH GREETING

1 Peter 1:1

Most letters written in first century began very simply: who the letter was from, who the letter was to, and a quick blessing. But, Peter's letters start a little differently.

Remember, he's was writing mostly to Christians who were Gentiles. Also remember, many Jewish people didn't believe that Gentiles were chosen by anyone or for anything. Certainly they were of no use to God!

But Peter wanted it to be clear that God's plan included Gentiles too. Can you imagine the hope they must have felt hearing those words? Can you appreciate the knowledge God must have given Peter for him to write those words?

A letter full of hope and rich in knowledge...that's how the letter that we call 1 Peter begins:

From Peter, a student of and a messenger for
Jesus Christ,
to the chosen pilgrims around the sea:

God knew all along you'd be His.
In fact, He chose you!
The Spirit is at work in you, making you holy,
and the way you live shows it.
Jesus's blood washed away all your sins,
so you can know God,
and to be changed by the Spirit.

Grace and peace to you.
More grace and more peace to you.
Even more grace and even more peace to you!

Kaleidoscope Corner
Peter's Faith Journey

From the time Jesus called Peter to follow Him, he had an unsteady, hot-or-cold faith. At Jesus's command, he walked on top of water. But when Peter looked away from Jesus to the rolling waves and stormy skies, he began to sink.

He listened to Jesus teach about His own coming death, but then pulled Jesus aside and told Him to stop talking! He ate food served to him by Jesus, but then shortly after, denied even knowing Jesus three times.

And even after all of that, God used Peter to build His Church, and to write part of the Bible.

In your Bible, read Matthew 14:22-33, Mark 8:31-33, Luke 22:54-62, and John 21:15-19. How did Peter's faith grow throughout his life? What helped his faith grow? As you read about Peter's two letters in the Bible, ask yourself: How did his time with Jesus shape what Peter wrote in his letters to early Christians?

HOPE IS ALIVE!

1 Peter 1:3-12

All praise to God, the Father of our Lord Jesus Christ!
Because of His great mercy, we are born again.
Because Jesus died, and lives again, we have a living hope!
This hope is perfect.
It won't rot.
It won't fade.
It's kept safe in heaven for you,
guarded like precious treasure.
It is our salvation,
and when the time is right,
it will be ours.

So rejoice!
Even though the trials that surround you right now don't
bring happiness, they prove your faith.
Just like gold stays gold through the hottest fire,
faith stays faith through the hardest trial.

Hope is what gets us through the times in life that are hard or sad. It's easy to put our hope in our family, or who our friends are, or the things we have, or the places we're going. We can see these things, but we can also lose them. Our true, living hope—the only hope that will really get us through hard or sad times—is in someone we can't see, but also can't lose.

Jesus gave up heaven to live on earth. He lived a perfect, sinless life, and died an unimaginably painful death. After three days, He defeated the grave, and rose from the dead. Why would God, in all His power and all His perfection, put Himself through all of this? Why did He do it?

For us. To save us. To be with us.

He died the death we deserve so that we can live the eternal life He deserved. Jesus is where we find our hope.

> You haven't seen Him, but you love Him.
> You can't see Him now, but you trust Him,
> and you laugh and sing
> even when the world doesn't understand.
>
> Because of His great mercy, you are alive.
> So you understand how
> what even the prophets didn't fully,
> and what angels wish they could understand:
> because of His holy love,
> you have joy now
> and hope in your salvation to come.

SO NOW...

1 Peter 1:13-2:3

So roll up your sleeves, children of God,
and let's get to work.
Because of God's grace that will be fulfilled on the
glorious day that Jesus returns,
you're not bossed around by the unholy things
you used to hope for.
Instead you practice self-control,
since your hope is in Him.

The self-control Peter writes about here is giving up what we want to go after what God wants. This isn't easy, and Peter's readers knew it then, just as we know it now. In fact, self-control is impossible on our own. That's why Peter goes on to write that the only way we can succeed is because of Jesus:

Remember what's been written before:
"Be holy, because I am holy."
Because He chose you,
and because He's holy,
you are also to be holy.
You know that the Perfect One
is the one you also call Father,
and you know that He will one day judge righteously,
so live with a holy fear of making Him unhappy.
As long as you're a pilgrim on this earth,
remember that your life was saved
not by things of this world,
but by the sacrifice of the perfect blood of Jesus.
God knew all along that He would send Jesus.
And because Jesus has made you His child,
your faith and hope are in God alone.

As naturally as two streams of water flowing together,
Peter moves from talking about how to live well with God
to encouraging readers to live well with one another.
These two are closely tied together!

Love each other.
Really, love each other!
Not with the weakness we have,
but with the power He gives us.

You see, we're all like grass.
And even at our loveliest?
We're the flowers that grow in the grass.

The grass will turn brown.
The flowers will die.
But God's Word is forever.

God's never-dying Word has been planted in your hearts,
so love each other with a never-dying love.
Get rid of hatred and meanness and lies and jealousy.
We have no need for them.
Be like babies, needing only the pure milk of His word.
The more you taste it, the more you know He's good,
and the more of Him you want.

WHAT GOD IS BUILDING

1 Peter 2:4-10

So you come to Him every day.
He was ignored by men, but chosen by God.
He's the cornerstone, the most important piece,
of the holy place God's building.
It will never crumble, and through Jesus,
you are part of it, as living stones.
Through Jesus, you are part of it,
as a holy priesthood.

Those who don't believe will see the cornerstone,
and stumble and fall.

But you—you are chosen.
You are royal.
You are holy.
You are His.

Tell of His goodness!
He has called you out of darkness,
into His beautiful light.

Peter paints a picture for his readers of God building a new temple, or holy house. In the Old Testament, the temple was where God lived, and only the high priest was allowed inside the holiest place to make sacrifices for the people. Even this only happened once each year.

This new temple isn't only for a few; it's for all who believe. And until Jesus comes back, the temple will keep growing as more "living stones" join what God is building. Together, the "stones"—Christians—are built into God's new temple. And together, Peter says that we are also the holy priesthood inside the temple.

Does this sound confusing? How can we be the stones that make up the building and also the priests inside? How can we be a holy place, and also do holy work?

It's only because of God's grace in sending Jesus and giving us the Spirit. Through God, we become much more than we could ever be on our own.

We belong to Him, and that doesn't just reorder how we live on our own, but it changes how we live together. We are connected to each other. The temple and the priesthood are made up of Christians before, Christians now, and Christians who will come after us. They may not look like us, speak our language, or worship God in the same way, but together, we are the new temple, and we are the new priests.

Once you were nothing, but now you are God's.
Once you were left to deal with your sin alone, but now God has given you mercy.

He has called you out of darkness,
into His beautiful light.

FREE SERVANTS

1 Peter 2:11-3:12

Dear friends, please, as chosen pilgrims here,
run away from the sin all around you.
Sin will start a war in your heart.

Instead, live such holy lives,
with all your hope in God and His goodness,
that those who don't know Jesus
will hear your words and see your actions,
and they will join you and praise God with you.

Listen to and obey your leaders and their laws.
God wants this.
Show that you obey God
by submitting to the leaders here on earth.
Real freedom comes from living as God's servants.
When you live like this,
even fools will have nothing left to say.
Honor everyone. Love each other.
Live in a holy fear of God.
Respect leaders and laws.

The world wants us to believe that we're in charge of ourselves. But being a Christian calls us to something more, and better.

We are called to submit to God in heaven, and to leaders here on earth. To submit is to know we aren't in charge, and to humbly let those who are in charge lead.

On the outside, submitting will look like obeying. And on the inside, submitting will feel like freedom: knowing our place as someone dearly loved and fully cared for by God.

But how can being a servant mean being free? It seems impossible. But, the same God who turned death around, and who turns lives around, can turn words around, too. And so, in God's turn-around kingdom, servants are free.

Some of you are servants.
Submit to your masters,
not only the good and kind ones,
but the mean ones too.
God sees and honors those who suffer unfairly.

If you do wrong, and are punished for it,
that's not suffering.
But if you do right, and are punished anyway,
that's suffering.
God will honor those who obey Him, and do good,
and still suffer.

Jesus is our example.
He never sinned. He only spoke love.
Yet on the cross, He took the punishment for our sins.
Because His body was broken, we are healed.
You wandered away like lost sheep,
but now you've come back to the Shepherd of your soul.

When Jesus's love changes us, it remakes every part of us. As followers of Jesus, we love, honor, and submit to God first. And we love, honor, and submit to people second.

If you're a wife, submit to your husband,
not only if he believes in Jesus, but also if he doesn't.
Perhaps he'll come to know Jesus
because of the way you live.

Your beauty doesn't come from the outside,
from perfect hair or fancy clothes,
but from a spirit that's gentle
and a heart that does good.

If you're a husband, honor your wife.
If you want your prayers to be heard by God,
treat her like who she is:
your equal partner in receiving God's blessing.

Finally, for all of you: be united in Christ.
Be kind. Keep your hearts soft and your minds humble.
Live in love.
If you want to love life and live good days,
don't lie or speak poorly.
Run away from evil. Do good.
Look for peace and work for it.
God sees the good you do, and hears your prayers,
but He's against those who do evil.

Kaleidoscope Corner
Slavery in the Bible

Peter writes to servants in chapter two. Some Bible translations use the word slaves here, and it's confusing to read this as Christians today. At the time Peter wrote this letter, most cultures had a form of servitude, or slavery, that was different from what we understand today as slavery.

Some people, including many early Christians, agreed to be servants in order to pay back money they owed, or to have a safe place to live. Many of the servants Peter wrote to were talented and educated: artisans, teachers, and even doctors. Most of them would have worked for a master for a certain amount of time, and would then earn back their freedom. No one ever hoped that one day they would be a servant! But because many early Christians were treated so poorly and often lost their jobs and homes, being a servant was what they had to do to have a place to live and food to eat.

Peter knew this, so he gave instructions to early Christians who were already servants. He did not say having or being servants was what God wanted. In fact, in 1 Corinthians 7:21, another early Church leader, Paul, teaches Christian servants that if they are able to earn their freedom, should do so right away.

So what does the Bible teach us about buying and selling people through slavery, based on the color of someone's skin?

That it was, and is, evil. Exodus 21:16 says "whoever steals a man and sells him, and anyone found in possession of him, shall be put to death."

And in the New Testament, Paul writes to Philemon, a slave owner, that his runaway slave, a new Christian, isn't actually a slave anymore, "but a beloved brother ...both in the flesh, and in the Lord."

In your Bible, read Genesis 1:26-27. What does this tell you about how God created all people? Then read Colossians 3:11. What has Jesus done to bring us together in unity? How do these verses make us certain that God is against slavery?

FAITH IN SUFFERING

1 Peter 3:13-22 & 4:12-19

If you are always ready to do good,
what's the worst that can happen?
You already know what your future holds in heaven,
Nothing, in all of creation, can take away that gift.

Peter reminded a group of Christians, who had suffered a
lot, that nothing they'd lost because of evil men could
compare to what they would gain because of their good
God:

Jesus, perfectly righteous,
suffered and died and rose again, to bring you to God.

So when you suffer because of your faith,
don't be surprised.
Jesus suffered, and when you share in His suffering,
the day He comes back will fill you with joy.

Like James, Peter heard Jesus teach. In the Sermon on the Mount, Jesus said, "Blessed are you when others revile you and persecute you and utter all kinds of evil against you falsely on My account. Rejoice and be glad, for your reward is great in heaven..." (Matthew 5:11-12).

Remember, Peter walked with Jesus and spoke with Jesus and ate with Jesus and heard Jesus teach. Peter was there when Jesus said these words. He knew that suffering for doing good is a part of being a Christian.

Peter also saw Jesus's miracles and watched Jesus die and saw Jesus risen again. So Peter also knew that no earthly suffering is forever, and that Jesus Himself is the ultimate reward.

When you're living God's way,
and you suffer,
trust Jesus, and trust His example.
Keep doing good,
and have faith in the One who is faithful.

TO LIVE GOD'S WAY

1 Peter 4:1-11

Think like Jesus, since He suffered as you suffer.
Leave sin behind.
Getting drunk, dishonoring your bodies,
and worshipping idols—
those days of living only for yourselves,
against God, are over.

Sinners will mock you for living God's way,
but they will answer to God
for their words and their actions.

Peter tells his readers in this section that in order to live God's way, they need to do two things. First, he tells them to leave behind their old lives of sin. And second, he tells them to love people deeply.

But, Peter lets them know that this won't come easily: he warns them that they'll be mocked for their choices. Yet God's way—the way of love—is worth it.

Practice self-control.
Keep your mind clear.
Most of all, love each other with everything you have.
Where love lives, sin is forgiven.

Welcome each other warmly,
and serve one another cheerfully.
Each of you has a gift. God gave it to you.
Take care of those gifts,
and use them to love each other:

if you speak, speak God's words, and
if you serve, serve God's way.
Then, in all that you do,
the glory will be God's through Jesus.

To Him be all glory and power forever and ever!

Kaleidoscope Corner
Doxologies

If you have learned about Psalms with Kaleidoscope, you might remember that a doxology is a short declaration of praise to God. These were—and often still are—sung together by God's people as hymns. We find these throughout the Bible, in the Old and New Testaments. 1 Peter has two of them:

- To Him be all glory and power forever and ever!
- The power and the glory are His! Forever and ever! Amen!

Doxologies were usually written at the end of books or letters, but not always. In your Bible, read Ephesians 3:20-21 and 1 Peter 4:11 and 5:10-11. Which parts of these verses are the doxologies? What truth about God caused Paul, the writer of Ephesians, to declare His praise in this passage? What truth about God caused Peter to declare His praise? What truth about God can you praise Him for today?

TO THE SHEPHERDS & THE SHEEP

1 Peter 5:1-11

To the shepherds:
you're the leaders of the Church,
and your responsibility is great.
Remember, you're not caring for your own sheep,
but for God's.
Serve because you want to, not because you have to.
Serve to give, not to get.
Lead by example, not just by words.
And when the Perfect Shepherd, Jesus, comes back,
a crown of glory will be yours forever.

Peter talks to the shepherds, or elders, of the Church here. He knows that those who lead won't have it easy: they will be held to higher standards. He also knows that the cost is worth it: the reward that's coming is better than anyone can imagine, and it will last forever.

So Peter reminds them: being a leader is about serving and loving. To love God, serve others. To love others, serve God.

Then Peter reminds everyone else that they have a job, too:

To the sheep:
listen to your shepherds.
God is against pride,
but He loves a humble heart.

At the time Peter was writing, telling someone to be humble was like telling someone now to be weak. No one wants to be called weak today, and no one in Peter's time wanted to be called humble. But in God's way of turning an upside-down, sinful world right-side up, a humble heart is a strong heart.

Think of humility as an orchestra following the conductor. The violinist could be the most talented in the world, but at a concert with an orchestra, if she ignored the conductor, and started playing whatever she wanted instead, she'd look foolish.

Or think of humility as a soccer team following the coach. Even the best players have to follow the direction of their coach in order to win. Being humble is knowing who we are in light of God's holiness. It's knowing how much we don't know. It's understanding how much we need our Savior and our King.

Then Peter finishes his first letter by reminding everyone what we should all do, and why:

To everyone:
be humble. Pray.
Every time you worry, tell God. He cares for you.
The enemy is like a hungry lion,
pacing while it waits to kill.
Don't be afraid. Stand tall in the power God has given,
and know that you're not alone.
Your family around the world suffers, too.

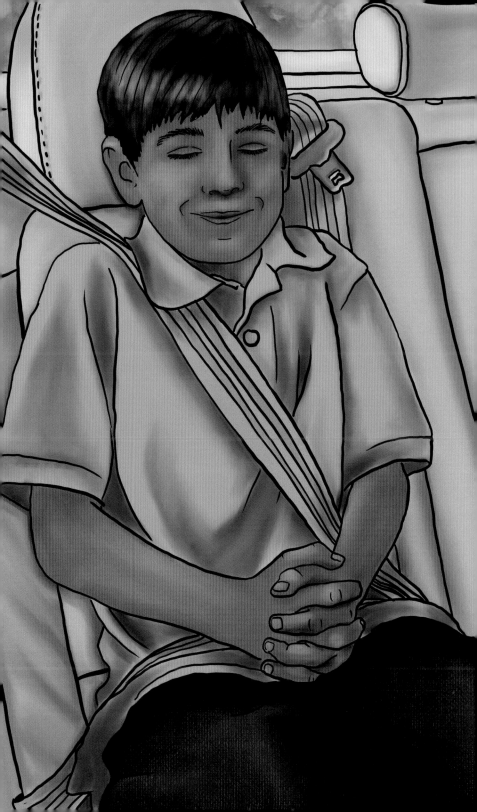

But after you have suffered a little while,
God, with His mighty hand—
the same mighty hand that delivered the Israelites out
of the darkness of slavery, and into the light of the
Promised Land—
will give you strength and power.
He will give you a name and a home.
He'll make everything right again.

The power and the glory are His!
Forever and ever!
Amen!

INTRODUCTION TO 2ND PETER

Dietrich Bonhoeffer, a pastor and teacher in Germany during the Second World War, was put in jail for speaking out against, and working to end, the evil rule of the Nazi government. During his time in jail, he prayed with and for himself and other prisoners, writing many of those prayers down:

> Now let me accept tribulation from Thy hand.
> Thou will not lay on me more than I can bear.
> Thou make all things work together for good for Thy children.

Bonhoeffer knew that taking a stand against evil leaders and evil laws would be costly. And two years after he was put in jail, he was killed by the Nazi government.

Two thousand years earlier, Peter knew that standing up to lying teachers and sinful living would be costly, as well.

A few years after he wrote his first letter, Peter wrote another, which we call 2 Peter. Look back to the map in the "Introduction to the First Letter of Peter." He was most likely writing to the same people as his first letter: early Gentile Christians around the Mediterranean Sea. This time, though, Peter wrote to them from jail.

Because he wrote it from jail, this letter feels different than Peter's first. Like his first letter, he still gives instructions and teaches about God, but with a different tone. You see, Peter knew he'd probably die soon. With every word he wrote to his readers, his brothers and sisters in the faith, he thought it might be his last. So he wrote this short, urgent letter to remind them of this: that God's grace, through Jesus, is what would give them the power to live holy lives of love, full of hope for the day when Jesus comes back.

Like you've already read, and also like James, Peter would eventually be killed for standing firm in his faith. He would lose his earthly life, but gain his eternal reward.

A SHORT GREETING

2 Peter 1:1-2

Peter knew he didn't have much time left, and also that he had more left to teach. So he opened his letter quickly to get right to what's most important.

From Simon Peter, a servant of Jesus Christ,
and a witness to His life,
to my brothers and sisters:
through Jesus's perfect saving grace,
your faith is as strong and beautiful as ours.
As you grow in your understanding of God,
may grace and peace grow around you.

GOD'S GRACE LEADS TO GODLINESS

2 Peter 1:3-15

Remember this:
because of God's grace, He lets us become more like Him.
Because of His power, you've escaped
the destruction sin causes.
Because of His calling, the best promises are ours:
the Holy Spirit,
Jesus's return,
and life forever with Him.

So here's what you need to do:
with everything you've got,
keep faith, and add goodness.
Keep goodness, and add knowledge.
Keep knowledge, and add self-control.
Keep self-control, and add courage.
Keep courage, and add godliness.
Keep godliness, and add warm friendship.
Keep warm friendship, and add love.

81

If you're growing in all of these ways, you won't fall.
You'll be fruitful
as you learn more about our King Jesus.

And the blessing that's coming
is a door into Jesus's forever kingdom.

I know my time here will be ending soon,
as Jesus has made clear to me,
so I want to make sure I've told you everything.

As Peter wrote this final letter from jail, it's clear that he remembered what Jesus told him years earlier: "'... when you are old you will stretch out your hands, and someone else will dress you and lead you where you do not want to go.' Jesus said this to share about the kind of death by which Peter would glorify God." (John 21:18-19)

Peter knew he would die soon, so writing everything down was one way to be sure every Christians would hear what God wanted to say through him, including us today!

Kaleidoscope Corner
God's Promises

In Chapter 2 of the book of Acts, Peter preached about three promises from God, and he points back to them here in his letter: the Holy Spirit to guide us, Jesus's return to bring the new heaven and earth, and eternal life to live with Him forever.

But those aren't the only promises of God's that we read about in the Bible.

In your Bible, read Genesis 9:8-17; Romans 6:14; 2 Corinthians 12:9; 1 John 1:9; and Psalm 50:15. What other promises are ours through Jesus?

THIS IS HOW WE KNOW

2 Peter 1:16-21

We didn't make any of this up.
We saw Jesus on the holy mountain,
shining brighter than the sun.
God wrapped Him in glory and honor, and
we heard Him say,
"This is my Son.
I love Him.
I'm delighted with Him."

Peter walked with Jesus and spoke with Him and ate with Him and heard Him teach and saw His miracles and watched Him die and rise again.

Peter also saw something awesome!

Actually it was *awesome*, as in wondrous and terrifying at the same time. Peter was a witness to Jesus's transfiguration. Peter, James, and John (the three "pillars," remember?) were with Jesus that day. They saw the holy and beautiful moment where Jesus was revealed as God.

At the time Peter wrote, some people accused the disciples of making the whole thing up. But Peter encouraged early Christians by telling them what he saw with his own eyes, and what he heard with his own ears. And then he reminded them about words that had already been written, in what we now call the Bible's Old Testament.

We've read what the prophets wrote,
words given to them by God,
proven true by Jesus's life.

So pay attention!
You're going to run into false teaching, into clever lies.
God's Truth shines like a lamp in a dark room,
while you wait for Jesus to return,
the sun rising on that beautiful morning.

A true prophecy doesn't come from men.
It comes from God, through the Holy Spirit.

The Old Testament of the Bible is filled with prophecy, or news about the Savior that would one day come. That prophecy came true through Jesus. The prophets were given these words—not just an idea or a thought or a picture in their minds, but the actual words—from God.

Peter teaches that God's Word is given by the Holy Spirit, written by men, and without mistakes. Through all of history, we know that some people have taken God's Word and used it to do wrong, claiming that the Bible says things it doesn't say, or that it means things it doesn't. This is because of human sin, and not because of God's perfect Word. Peter makes sure we understand that every single word in the Bible matters, because every tiny syllable is the truth from God.

Kaleidoscope Corner
The Bible

Have you ever wondered where the Bible comes from? It's is a collection of many different letters, stories, and poems written throughout history in many different times and places, by many different men. Before most people could read or write, books were rare. So, many early Christians never even saw a written copy of the Bible, and certainly most of them never read one themselves.

But by the middle of the 1400s, when the printing press was invented, books became easier to make and get, so more people learned to read. Christians at that time knew that if many copies of God's Word could be printed, then more and more people would be able to read it, and experience the story: the greatest story ever told. It's the story of creation, sin, grace, redemption, and glory. It's the story of God, and what He's done—and is doing—for people like us.

Early in the history of the Christian Church, a group of leaders and scholars decided what to include in the Bible. Over many years, and after many disagreements, the Bible became the 66 books we know today.

They called the final copy "the canon." Canon comes from a Greek word that means "a measuring stick, or ruler," and that's why we use the word now to mean "a rule or standard." The canon includes ancient history books, poetry and songs of praise, books of law, prophecy books, the story of Jesus, and letters like James and 1 and 2 Peter.

THE DANGER OF FALSE TEACHERS

2 Peter 2:1-22

There are false prophets and teachers,
who won't take direction or instruction or correction
from anyone.
They'll even deny the Creator, who made them
in His own image.

But God will act justly.
After all, if God drowned His own creation in a flood,
but saved Noah and his family,
and if God destroyed evil cities,
but saved Lot, who was faithful,
then know this:

God will take care of the wicked in judgement,
and He will rescue the faithful.

Sometimes false teachers are easy to recognize, and sometimes it's trickier.

Many false teachers say or do things that are so evil, you can spot them from a mile away.

But what if a teacher tells a lie that sounds right or feels good? What if that false teacher even uses words from the Bible to convince people their words are true?

Peter warned early Christians to be careful when choosing who to listen to. But he also told them to rest in this: God is the final judge, and He will hold false teachers accountable for what they've said and done. We need to be careful who we listen to and learn from.

You already know that people who don't know Jesus are ruled by the sins of the world.

But I'm telling you, it's worse for someone
to know about Jesus and His love,
and to still choose to go back to sin.
They knew what was good and true and beautiful,
and then still turned back to evil and lies and ugliness.
They're like freshly cleaned pigs who roll in filth,
and dogs who lick up their own vomit.
Gross!!!

Peter, writing from jail, shares an important warning here: those who only *pretend* to follow Jesus will return to their old ways of sin. God will hold them responsible for knowing the truth, but instead choosing to go back, time and time again, to lies.

But for those who not only know *about* Jesus, but who also *know* Jesus, and who live in His perfect love, the best of life is still to come!

THE LORD'S DAY IS COMING

2 Peter 3:1-13

When you're learning something new, you don't know everything there is to know right away. And even after we know something, it doesn't mean we always remember it. We all need reminding. So, Peter begins the last section of his second letter with an important reminder: what we believe about the future matters, and what we believe about the future changes how we live now.

Dear family, remember this:
the Lord's day is coming!

Fools and evil ones will laugh and mock,
"Where is the one who made all these promises?
Asleep?"
They ignore all the promises He's already kept:
He created the water,
and then used it to flood
and destroy the evil in His world.

Remember His promises.
He won't break them. Never has. Never will.

Peter reminds his readers that they shouldn't doubt what the Lord has promised about the day He's coming back. We know all of His promises are true, even when they're hard to understand.

Remember when Noah was alive and God used something He made, water, to flood His own creation, because it was filled with evil? That's confusing, but God's plan was perfect and just what was needed at just the right time!

God promises that fools and evil ones will face His judgement. So don't ignore or make light of the coming day of the Lord. For people who don't know Jesus, it will be a terrifying day, far beyond their worst nightmares. But for those of us who love Jesus, it will be a great, glorious day, far beyond our most beautiful dreams.

Peter's instructions here are clear: we are to prepare for the next life during this one. For those of us who know Him, we can be full of hope, and live holy and right lives now, knowing that the best is yet to come!

He's not slow.
He is patient.
He is good.
He wants you to live as you were created.
So every minute He gives you
is a chance to live in His love.

Because He promised it,
we are waiting for the Lord's day,
for the new heavens and the new earth,
where His beauty and glory live.

Kaleidoscope Corner
Therefore

Any time you read the word *therefore* in the Bible, ask yourself: what's the *therefore* there for? It's a connecting word that links the Scripture before it with the Scripture after it. Often, there's information about God before the *therefore*, followed by instructions on how to live after it. Peter does that here, connecting all that he taught his readers about God in 3:1-13, with his final instructions for them in 3:14-18.

In your Bible, read 1 Peter 3:1-18. What does Peter teach us about God in the first part of the chapter? What does he remind us to do? How are those two answers connected?

UNTIL THEN...

2 Peter 3:14-18

Therefore,
my dear family, while you're waiting,
spend your time here wisely.
Don't be corrupted by false teachers,
but work to be pure in heart and mind.

Grow in what you know about Jesus,
and grow in knowing Jesus.
He is our Lord and Savior,
and gets all our glory,
now and forever.
Amen.